The Aligned Teacher:

A Guide to Sanity When You Just Want to Quit

By
Meredith Ruben Daniels

www.soulful-wellness.com

Copyright © 2023 Meredith Ruben Daniels

All rights reserved.

All rights reserved. No part of this book may be reproduced or used in any manner without the prior written permission of the copyright owner, except for the use of brief quotations in a book review.

Edited by Barbara Williams

Disclaimer: This book does not replace medical or mental health advice. Consult your doctor or mental health professional for serious concerns.

DEDICATION

To Kevin, for making a difference in the lives of your students and your family

And

To all teachers, who dedicate their lives to making our world a better place through our children

Table of Contents

DEDICATION v
ACKNOWLEDGEMENTS ix
1 Welcome, Wonderful Teachers! 11
2 Energy and Emotions 17
3 Am I an Empath? 21
4 The Central Dig 25
5 The Cross Over and DNA Spiral 29
    The Cross Over 29
    The DNA Spiral 30
6 The Hook Up 31
7 Triple Warmer Smoothie 33
8 Emotional Freedom Technique 35
9 Bubble of Peace 1.0 37
10 Bubble of Peace 2.0 39
11 Meditation 41
12 Gratitude 45
13 Visualization and Manifestation 49
14 Essential Oils 53
    Essential Oil Recommendations: 56
    Safety Tips: 57
15 Grounding 61

16	Stomping in the Grass	63
17	Salt	65
18	Feng Shui	67
19	Acupressure Points	71
20	Breathwork	73
21	Crystals	77
	Where should I get my crystals?	80
22	Sound Healing	81
23	Forest Bathing	85
24	Final Thoughts	89
RESOURCES		91
ABOUT THE AUTHOR		93

ACKNOWLEDGEMENTS

A very special thanks to Marilyn Eagen, Donna Eden, Jen Mavros, Abraham Hicks, Dr. Jeffrey Long, Gina Ballard, Brad Yates, Michelle Woodruff, Dr. Stefanie Sanger Woollen, Dr. Rebecca Sturmer, April Wollard, Gina Ballard, Michael Abney, and many others for sharing your knowledge with me and guiding me on my spiritual journey.

Welcome, Wonderful Teachers!

I am so grateful for you and all the amazing work you do in the lives of kids! Teaching has always had its challenges, but the times we are currently living in have multiplied those challenges exponentially. It is a lot for anyone to handle, even the most experienced teachers. Unfortunately, due to a number of reasons, we are seeing a huge amount of teachers burning out and leaving the profession. While I am a firm believer that everyone should do what is right for them, it is also disheartening to see children take the hit. My goal with this book is to give you some tools to help you feel more balanced and aligned; to manage your stress levels more effectively; to show up as the best YOU for your students, your family, and yourself; and to be happy to stay in the career you love.

Before we get into the fun part, allow me to introduce myself. My name is Meredith Ruben Daniels. I wanted to be a kindergarten teacher ever since I was in kindergarten myself. All of my jobs

The Aligned Teacher

growing up involved working with kids - camp counselor, Sunday School assistant, pre-ballet class assistant. I went on to receive my B.S. in Elementary Education from the University of Wisconsin-Madison and my Master of Arts in Teaching from Missouri Baptist University. I was hired to teach kindergarten the day before school started in 2006. I spent 9 years in the classroom, including both elementary and early childhood settings. I absolutely adored my students, but the Universe kept showing me signs that I wasn't supposed to be in the classroom.

While in college, I was fortunate enough to do a month-long teaching practicum at Yeo Park Infants School in Sydney, Australia. The school was literally an old house in the middle of a park, right out of a fairy tale. It was a K-2 school with only 3 classes, and the kindergarten teacher doubled as the principal. When the practicum ended, my parents and boyfriend (now husband), Kevin, came to visit and we traveled the country for two weeks. We went to the Sydney Opera House, hiked around Uluru and snorkeled at the Great Barrier Reef.

The day we were supposed to fly home, my mom, Kevin and I went to mail home a souvenir that we couldn't carry on the plane while my Dad stayed behind at the hotel to pack. Upon returning to the hotel, we knocked on the door for my Dad to let us in.

There was no answer.

Meredith Ruben Daniels

When the hotel staff let us in the room, we found my Dad sitting on the couch, unresponsive. After hours at the hospital, we found out that he had suffered a brain hemorrhage, and there was no way to save him. We had to say goodbye.

My Dad's passing was the catalyst for my spiritual journey. Dr. Jeffrey Long's book, Evidence of the Afterlife: The Science of Near Death Experiences, solidified my belief that life continues beyond our physical existence and that the signs my Dad was sending me were actually from him. Taking part in psychic readings and attending spiritual classes and retreats led to me becoming a Reiki Master, a certified Generational Emotional Mapping (GEM) Ancestral Healer, and discovering my own gift as a Psychic Medium. Along the way, I have learned many tips and tricks for aligning my energy and I thought these might be helpful for you as well!

I am married to my high school sweetheart, Kevin, who is a phenomenal high school math teacher. Kevin has an incredible gift for relating to his students to the point of having students ask him to adopt them. He has worked almost exclusively with at-risk students in the school for his entire career, and even volunteered to be the math teacher for a special program providing extra support to those students with dire needs. This commitment allowed for only one advanced class a day to provide some balance. While he made a tremendous impact on his students, I have watched how it affected him at home. Kevin would come home stressed out every day. He got migraines often, and would come home, go straight to the bedroom, turn off the lights, and have to decompress before he could participate in our family's evening activities. He thought about his students constantly, and their troubles weighed heavily upon him. His teammates experienced health issues, as well, and talked often about their nightly crutches to decompress from the day.

Teachers play instrumental roles in the lives of their students, and caring about them and thinking about them when you are "off the clock" comes naturally. But in seeing how this stress impacted every area of Kevin's life, I knew that other teachers had to be struggling, too. Teachers give so much of themselves, and while teaching is a huge part of who they are, they deserve to have happy lives with their families and friends, without the weight of their students or the demands of school constantly upon their shoulders.

While it has been a minute since I've personally been in the classroom, I remember how stressful it can be at times. This book contains tips and tricks that can help you balance your energy and reduce your stress levels, allowing you to feel better physically, mentally and emotionally. I have done everything in the book myself, and have given Kevin a routine to follow with many of these tips, as well. As a bonus, many of these exercises can even be done with your students to help them feel better, too!

Just like in teaching, I am giving you many strategies. Do not feel

Meredith Ruben Daniels

like you need to do all of them in order to feel better. Take what works for you and leave the rest.

Thank you for all you do to impact the lives of kids. You are a superhero and deserve to feel peace and happiness in all areas of your life.

Energy and Emotions

When people hear the word "energy," a lot of them think of it as being "woo woo," weird, or something that is only for spiritual hippies. But if you ask any science teacher, they will tell you that energy is, in fact, a real scientific concept that has many forms (potential, kinetic, thermal, etc.), including some forms that the scientific community has not yet quantified. Every single thing on Earth has energy, including people, animals, plants and even your kitchen table. Try this: briskly rub your hands together for a minute and then slowly separate them. You will be able to feel the energy between your hands.

Each individual is surrounded by their own personal energy field. This field vibrates at a rate specific to you and how you are feeling. When you are feeling joy, peace, love, or any other "positive" emotion, your energy is vibrating at a faster rate, also referred to as a high vibration. You know those shirts and mugs that say "Good vibes only" or "high vibe"? This is what they're referring to. If a person is feeling sad, angry, anxious, or fearful, their energy vibrates at a much slower rate, also referred to as a low vibration.

It is possible to change your vibration by changing your emotions. Below is a list from Abraham Hicks that shows how various emotions rank in terms of vibration, with the lowest vibrating emotions at the bottom and the highest vibrating emotions at the top.

Joy/Appreciation/Empowered/Freedom/Love
Passion
Enthusiasm/Eagerness/Happiness
Positive Expectation/Belief
Optimism
Hopefulness
Contentment
Boredom
Pessimism
Frustration/Irritation/Impatience
Overwhelm
Disappointment
Doubt
Worry
Blame
Discouragement
Anger
Revenge
Hatred/Rage
Jealousy
Insecurity/Guilt/Unworthiness
Fear/Grief/Depression/Despair/Powerlessness

Meredith Ruben Daniels

As a teacher (and as a human), it is quite common to feel emotions all over this scale. While we can feel a variety of emotions every day, we each have a general emotional set point, which is where our emotions lie when nothing extreme is happening in our lives. When you started teaching, you most likely had a lot of emotions high on the scale as most new teachers are extremely optimistic and thrilled for their chance to change the world one student at a time (YAY for new teacher optimism!!). While many more experienced teachers still have their love and passion for teaching, it is common for teachers to feel overwhelmed, worried, disappointed, fearful and even powerless. There are many situations that you simply cannot control. In the world of Covid and its aftermath, these emotions are likely to be amplified even more. While it is difficult to jump from the bottom of the scale straight to the top, consistent effort can help you climb through the emotional scale one rung at a time.

Experiencing these lower vibrating emotions on a regular basis can create a variety of difficult situations, including the manifestation of physical and mental health problems and inability to enjoy your life both inside and outside of school. If you feel the need to have a drink after work every night to unwind from the day; have trouble sleeping on Sunday night in anticipation of Monday morning; come home from work in tears or wonder how much longer you can do this, you are sitting lower on the emotional scale. If you find yourself here, please do not judge yourself for it. This does not make you "bad," but objectively observing where you are can help you see where to

The Aligned Teacher

make changes in your life. I am hopeful that the information you are about to read will help you embrace your ability to move higher up on the scale.

That's not the end of the story with energy, though. Our amazing science teachers can also tell us that energy is able to transfer from one object to another. When you play pool, the energy of you pushing the cue transfers to the ball that you hit, which then transfers to the next ball that is hit. It's all the same energy that keeps getting passed around.

The same thing happens with people. We all have the ability to absorb the energy of those around us. People who are strong in this ability are called empaths.

Am I an Empath?

As a teacher, you most likely try to instill empathy in your students, teaching them that it's important to care about others or to try to walk a mile in someone else's shoes. But what does it mean to be an empath?

An empath is a person who picks up on other people's energy and takes it on as their own, oftentimes unaware that they are doing this. The vast majority of teachers are empaths, whether they know it or not.

Let me give you an example. I was up late one night scrolling through social media, when I happened upon a video of a high school dance team doing a flash mob. The video showed a woman watching in the crowd, her chin resting in her hand, looking like her mind was somewhere else. All of a sudden, her boyfriend joined the flash mob.

The Aligned Teacher

The woman freaked out - she started jumping up and down and screaming. After showing off some moves, the woman's boyfriend had her come down to the gym floor, got down on one knee and proposed. The woman started crying and said yes! While watching this video, I felt my own emotions start to swell inside me - I was smiling, felt warm, and shed my own tears by the end of the video. I was so happy for this adorable couple, and they are complete strangers to me! I wasn't even there in person, but could feel their energy through the video and shared in their joy to the point of having a physical and emotional reaction myself.

While being an empath in happy situations is great (and often overlooked), it can be challenging to be around people who are sad, angry or fearful. When you think about a mob mentality, people easily join in angry shouting or violence because that energy is spreading throughout the crowd and people are absorbing it as their own without realizing that it doesn't belong to them.

As a teacher, you are constantly surrounded by other people. You have students who are frustrated as they struggle with academics, have problems with friends, or have difficult home situations. They bring all of this to school and oftentimes, dump it in your lap. Even if they don't share what's going on with you, you can still feel it in their energy or see it in their behavior. At lunch, there might be teachers complaining or venting in the teachers' lounge. Perhaps you have an administrator who is having a rough time and takes it out on the teachers, possibly even on the day of your evaluation. All of these emotions are hitting you at once, and if you don't know how to protect your energy, they are getting stuck in your energy field without you realizing it and bringing you down, too.

Think about a time when you got bad news. What happened to your body? Chances are, your heart rate increased; your palms became sweaty; your stomach tied in knots; and you may have searched for the nearest bathroom. This is a simple example of how our emotions affect our physical bodies in moments of stress. If you allow other people's emotions to take over your own on a consistent basis, adding to your own stress, they are going to eventually manifest into something physical, such as chronic illness, pain, disease, or depression. The vast majority of our physical ailments began as emotions first. Even if you have an injury from an accident, stuck emotions can cause the injury to persist. Thanks to epigenetics, we know that when we are able to change our emotions and beliefs, we are able to change the presentation of our genetics, resulting in healthier, happier lives.

As the loving, empathic teacher you are, chances are it is difficult for you to leave school at school. You not only bring home papers to grade or your lesson plans to work on, but you also bring home your emotions. You think about the student who doesn't have a warm winter coat; wonder if another has food for dinner; or if they are getting enough attention from their parents who travel and leave them with the nanny all the time. You may even turn on the news to see your students arrested for gang activity and shootings. You got into teaching because of your big heart, and it is easy to focus all of your energy on worrying about these students.

Teachers have been dealing with these issues since the beginning of education, and then we threw Covid into the mix. No matter where you fall on your views on Covid, there has been a lot of fear and anxiety added to our daily lives.

While pouring your heart and soul into your teaching is wonderful, admirable and so very appreciated by caregivers, you deserve not to have to carry the weight of the world on your shoulders at all times. When you come home from school, are you energized or exhausted? Do you look forward to spending time with your own family or do you need time to decompress from the day? Do you feel the need to have a glass of wine or overindulge in food every night in order to relax and unwind? If so, I would like to help you find some healthy ways to manage your energy and your stress level so that you can feel more centered, grounded, and happy. When your energy is aligned, you will be better able to show up for both yourself and your loved ones.

Following are my favorite tips and tricks for balancing, aligning and protecting your energy. As I stated earlier, you do not need to do every single tip for this to work. Try each one a few times and see what works best for you.

The Central Dig

The Central Dig is an exercise I learned from my Shaman/Reiki Master, Marilyn Eagen. This is an exercise that everyone should do first thing in the morning to help balance their energy and make sure they are centered and grounded to start their day. It can be repeated throughout the day as needed. The Central Dig works with the Central Vessel meridian (meridians are energetic pathways that run throughout the body in the skin and fascia), which is a line of hypnosis that goes up the center of your body. It also opens up the spleen meridian, which allows us to adapt to stressors that we are exposed to so we can calm down easier. Further, it allows the aura to attach to the body for protection and opens up a point in the bottom of the feet that helps us ground (more on grounding later). This exercise corrects so many things that commonly get misaligned in your energy field. If you only do one thing in this whole book, this should be it!

The Aligned Teacher

This is a great exercise to do with your students at your morning meeting or the beginning of your class. Here are the steps:

1. Stand with your feet firmly planted on the ground.

2. Using the middle two to three fingers on each hand, you are going to make gentle wiggle/digging motions up the center of your body. Begin at hip level and alternate each hand, one on top of the other, as you work your way up past your navel, heart, and neck. With each dig, say the words, "I am safe." Try to say it out loud, but you can say it to yourself if necessary.

3. Once you get to your chin, hold onto it with one hand.

4. While holding onto your chin, use your other hand to gently dig at the base of your skull in the little groove at the top of the back of your neck. Visualize your energy coming up from your tailbone through your spine to meet your hand. Dig and say, "I am safe" three to four times here.

5. Continue holding onto your chin and bring your other hand up to the top of your head. Wiggle and say, "I am safe" three to four times in this position.

6. Take a deep breath and relax.

7. If you would like, you can repeat this exercise using different phrases. "I am peace," "I am ease," "I am love," or "I am fun" are all great choices depending on what you need at the moment.

The Cross Over and DNA Spiral

We are at our healthiest and most vibrant when our energy is aligned to crisscross patterns. Even our DNA spirals and crosses over itself. Unfortunately, we do a lot of activities on a daily basis that make our bodies resonate to more linear patterns or straight lines. When we are on a linear pattern, our energy is only functioning at around fifty percent, which makes us more susceptible to illness. Marilyn Eagen also taught me the Cross Over and DNA Spiral, exercises which will help keep your energy crisscrossing and swirling to keep you healthy, energetic and strong. They help to balance and activate your crossover pattern throughout all levels of your energy system.

The Cross Over

1. Put your right hand on your left shoulder.

2. Firmly pull your hand down and across your body so that it sweeps off your right hip. This will make the first line of an X shape across your torso. Repeat with your left hand on your right shoulder.

3. Do this multiple times.

4. As you do this, visualize yourself wiping off any unwanted energy, stress, or energy that does not belong to you.

The DNA Spiral

1. Using 2 fingers, reach down towards the ground for the energy beneath your toes.

2. While visualizing a DNA helix, spiral your fingers up your body to above the top of your head, going whichever direction feels natural.

3. When you reach the top, reverse the direction of your fingers and spiral them back down towards the ground.

4. Repeat this three to seven times.

The Hook Up

The Hook Up is an Eden Energy Medicine exercise. This is a great exercise to do after you've lost it and need to pull yourself back together, or you can do it preemptively to help you not lose it to begin with! It helps you feel centered and grounded when in a stressful situation. On a physical level, the Hook Up helps reconnect your nervous system, making this a great exercise to do if you are feeling dizzy or just "off."

This is a wonderful exercise to have students do at morning meeting, before a test, or if they are upset and need help calming down. Make sure to teach this while the kids are calm before using it to help de-escalate a situation.

1. Place one finger in your belly button.

The Aligned Teacher

2. Place one finger on your third eye (the middle of your forehead).

3. Pull both fingers up gently and take at least three deep breaths. You can find a link to a video demonstration of the Hook Up in the Resources section at the end of this book.

Triple Warmer Smoothie

The Triple Warmer Smoothie is another Eden Energy Medicine exercise for instant stress relief. You might be curious about the funny name - Triple Warmer is the energy meridian in the body that controls the fight, flight, or freeze response. When activated, the body produces adrenaline and anxiety, causing a lot of uncomfortable feelings both physically and emotionally. The Triple Warmer Smoothie calms the triple warmer meridian, reducing stress hormones, allowing the body to relax and the brain to use higher executive thinking.

Use Triple Warmer Smoothie to keep yourself calm in stressful situations. Doing this will not only help you feel better in the moment, but will also reduce the amount of stress that will accumulate in your body and keep you physically, mentally and emotionally healthier over time.

The Aligned Teacher

This is an excellent exercise to teach your students. They can do this before a test, if having a conflict with a friend, or if they are feeling overwhelmed by a new concept they don't understand.

1. Place your hands gently over your eyes.

2. Gently drag your fingers to your temples.

3. Take a deep breath, then drag your fingers up and around your ears, down your neck, and hang your hands on your shoulders.

4. Take another deep breath, press your fingers into your shoulders, and drag them down to meet over your heart, breathing deeply again.

You can find a video demonstration of the Triple Warmer Smoothie in the Resources section of this book.

Emotional Freedom Technique

The Emotional Freedom Technique, also known as EFT or Tapping, is a technique that has been clinically proven in over 100 peer-reviewed papers to reduce anxiety, depression, PTSD, pain, phobias, and many other physical and emotional ailments. EFT rewires the neural pathways in your brain to change your limiting beliefs, fears, traumas, or other patterns that are holding you back from the life you want to live.

Emotional Freedom Technique involves tapping your fingers on a series of acupressure points on your body while talking through your issues. While I have done EFT several times myself, I am not an expert in it. I do know, however, that it is an effective tool for stress relief and mental and emotional health, so I wanted to make sure you could add it to your tool belt if it resonates with you.

The Aligned Teacher

While there are many videos you can find online about Emotional Freedom Technique, my favorite is Brad Yates. Brad has a YouTube channel with hundreds of videos on a vast number of topics to tap about. Some of his topics include: fear of Covid, achieving desired outcomes, money mindset, health topics, overcoming past trauma, overthinking, and so much more. This is a great place to start - simply search through his videos to find some that resonate for you.

If you have specific issues that you would like personalized support with, I highly recommend reaching out to a certified EFT specialist, such as my friend, Michelle Woodruff. Michelle is a certified EFT practitioner and will be able to help you on a more individualized basis. Michelle's sessions are virtual, so anybody can meet with her. If you would like to meet with Michelle, her information is in the Resources section at the end of this book.

Bubble of Peace 1.0

I learned the Bubble of Peace from my Hypnobabies natural childbirth class, but I use it all the time in my daily life. The Bubble of Peace allows you to create an energetic barrier between you and anything negative or unwanted in your environment. This technique helps you to be an objective observer of the outside world as opposed to being an active participant who is having negative or stressful reactions to what is going on around you. Remember, even if someone is attacking you, their words and actions are a reflection of what they are going through, not a reflection of you personally. When we are able to step back and observe this, rather than taking it as a personal attack, we are able to show more empathy for the other person and find objective ways to solve the problem using higher order thinking. Being able to demonstrate calm reactions to stressful situations is a wonderful example to set for your students and family.

The Aligned Teacher

What a wonderful lesson to teach that violence and anger are not the only responses to stress and negativity! Close your eyes if you prefer.

1. Imagine a bubble surrounding you. Visualize what color it is, how thick it is, if there are any sparkles, stripes, or anything special in it. Maybe it looks like a disco ball, reflecting everything from outside back out away from you.

2. Visualize things that you love and make you feel good inside your bubble - this could be a loved one, your bed, your favorite cozy blanket, etc. Only things that make you feel good and peaceful are allowed inside your bubble! Anyone or anything that causes you stress (even if you love them), are not allowed inside your bubble. Who you allow inside can change on a daily basis.

3. At the beginning of your day or before entering a stressful situation (your evaluation with your principal; the teacher's lounge with the drama queen coworkers; that one class of the day with the worst behaved students...), say to yourself, "Bubble of Peace." Instantly, your bubble will appear around you and you will feel a sense of calm rush over you. You are the observer and realize that other people's behavior has nothing to do with you, it has everything to do with them and how they perceive the world.

10

Bubble of Peace 2.0

If you want to take your Bubble of Peace to the next level, here is a fun little twist for you! Adding essential oils can amplify the protection level of your Bubble of Peace. We'll talk more about essential oils later, but I'll give you a sneak peek now.

Essential oils have emotional properties that can help us feel certain ways or release specific emotions. dōTERRA Essential Oils offers several blends that are helpful for protecting your energy.

dōTERRA's Terrashield blend is most often used as a bug repellent. Emotionally, however, it helps repel negative energy. This is a great oil to use if you are dealing with bullies (kids or adults), negative coworkers, unpleasant relatives, etc.

dōTERRA's On Guard blend is best known for its immune system support, but emotionally is a wonderful oil for protection. If you feel like you are vulnerable, at risk of attack, or you are scared of getting hurt, On Guard is a great oil to help you feel protected.

1. Put a drop of Terrashield or On Guard (or a drop of each) in the palm of your hand and rub your hands together. Without actually touching your face, cup your hands over your nose and mouth and deeply inhale the scent of the oil.

2. Visualize your Bubble of Peace.

3. Wave your hands around your entire body, picturing yourself painting the oil onto your bubble. If you feel a little silly doing this, close the door to your room and do it where nobody can see you. Or you can have a bubble party with your kids or spouse in the morning before you leave the house!

Meditation

Meditation is the practice of calming and clearing your mind. If you do not currently meditate, the word might bring to mind monks sitting on a mountainside, but meditation is truly for everyone. To be able to sit in peace and quiet, with no distractions, and just enjoy the silence, is a beautiful thing. It allows you to take a deep breath, to connect with your body and your breathing, and not think about your to-do list or whatever you are worrying about at the time. Meditation shifts your brain waves into a theta state, which promotes calm and relaxed feelings, as well as promoting creativity and spiritual connection. Everybody deserves to have a few minutes of peace and quiet to themselves every day!

There are a variety of well documented health benefits to meditation. Some of these include reducing stress levels, controlling anxiety, increasing emotional health, enhancing self-awareness, lengthening attention span, reducing age-related memory loss, generating kindness and positive feelings, helping to fight addictions, improving sleep, controlling pain, and decreasing blood pressure.

A lot of people think meditation isn't for them because they have a hard time sitting still. If this is you, don't worry - there are lots of ways to meditate! Meditation is a practice, not a destination, meaning when you do it on a regular basis, you will get better at it, but it will vary from day to day. If you can only start off with 30 seconds, that's great! The next day, try 45 seconds, then a minute. Even with a regular practice, some days will be easier than others.

The following is a list of different types of basic meditation. There are more involved forms of meditation that are not listed here that you can research further if you like. Find the one that feels best to you and start there.

1. Calming Meditation involves simply sitting in a quiet place, closing your eyes, and focusing on your breath, a mantra, or the sensations in your body. If a thought comes into your mind, you simply allow it to float away. You can do this in silence or play relaxing meditation music - a quick internet search will help you find lots of options.

2. Guided Meditation is when you listen to someone guide you through a meditation. This is a great alternative for people who

have a hard time quieting their mind on their own. Guided meditations will often have you picture a scenario - walking through a forest, floating down a river, etc. Once again, you can find many guided meditations online. If you feel called, I have a free guided meditation on my website called "Put Your Worries Down," which you can find in the Resources section of this book.

3. Moving Meditation is wonderful for people who don't like to sit still. You can be in a meditative state while moving your body. The best way to do this is personal to you. Moving meditation can be going for a walk in nature, running, swimming, doing yoga, or any movement that brings you peace. It can also include activities such as painting, drawing, sewing, etc. The important thing is that you do not get caught up in doing the activity perfectly, but relax in the movement of it.

4. Mini Meditation is perfect for when you are short on time. You can do this between classes, on your lunch break, waiting for copies, or even in the bathroom. Simply press each finger, one at a time, to the thumb on the same hand, starting with your pointer finger and working toward your pinky. As you gently press your fingertips together, say either out loud or in your head, "I am peace" or any other mantra you would like to say with each touch. Feel the peace inside of you as you do this. You can repeat this as many times as you wish. This is a great one to do with your students.

Gratitude

Practicing gratitude is one of the best things you can do to make yourself feel better and change your situation. Choosing to find the good in your life and being grateful for it can instantly raise your vibration. It is impossible to feel fear and gratitude at the same time, so when we choose gratitude, it forces our negative feelings to go away, even if just for that moment. The trick is to not just say the words, but to really FEEL the gratitude in your heart and in your body.

Every single person has things in their life to be grateful for. We can start with the obvious family and friends. Pick out one person and truly think about why you are grateful for them. Do they make you laugh? Did they help you through a difficult situation? Do you love the smell of their hair or the way it feels when you hug them?

What about your home? Did it keep you warm and dry during a

The Aligned Teacher

storm? Do you have a favorite spot that makes you feel safe and cozy? What about your bed and the feeling of crawling under the covers after a long day? Even something as little as your toothbrush is something to be grateful for - if you've ever had to go more than a day without brushing your teeth, you have certainly felt gratitude for your toothbrush!

There are several ways to practice gratitude:

1. Feel it in the moment as it is happening. Placing your hand on your heart and taking a deep breath to breathe in the moment is a nice addition.

2. At dinner every night, talk or think about three things you were grateful for that day. Knowing this discussion is coming forces you to notice positive moments throughout the day so you are prepared to share them that night.

3. Keep a gratitude journal. You can do this however you want, but here are a few suggestions:
   a. Write 3-5 things you are grateful for every morning when you wake up to start your day with gratitude.
   b. Write 3-5 things you are grateful for every night before bed to reflect on the good in your day.

   c. Choose one thing each day, and write 5-10 reasons why you are grateful for it (this helps you hone in on the actual feeling of gratitude).

4. If you have a difficult situation in your life, focus on the positive aspects of the situation, like what it is teaching you or what skills you are gaining to be able to deal with it.

When someone is really getting under your skin, whether it's a student, a coworker, a family member, etc., make a list of that person's positive attributes (yes, they have some, even if you really have to dig to find them). Read over your list before you see that person. If they are really annoying you, remind yourself of the items on the list. When you purposely choose to see the good in someone, you will see more of it, just like when you look for things to be grateful for, more things to be grateful for will show up in your life. If you want to establish gratitude as a habit, make signs or sticky notes to put in places you will see them - perhaps your car, the bathroom mirror or your desk, asking "What are you grateful for in this moment?" Making a large sign to put in your classroom will provide a wonderful discussion topic for your students and provide them with a daily reminder, as well.

Visualization and Manifestation

Visualization is a powerful tool used by the top athletes, CEOs, and successful people all over the world. Olympic athletes use visualization to picture themselves sticking their landing and waving from the podium, feeling the weight of their gold medal around their necks. CEOs visualize themselves signing the big business deal and celebrating with a lobster dinner on a tropical island. When you have a goal or something you desire, seeing it in your mind helps it to become real. This activates the universal Law of Attraction. The Law of Attraction states that what you focus on must manifest in your reality. You are utilizing the Law of Attraction every second of every day, whether you know it or not.

I know a lot of people who seem to have one thing after another go wrong. Are they consciously asking for this? Of course not! The secret to the Law of Attraction is that the Universe doesn't respond to

The Aligned Teacher

your words, it responds to your vibration. Every situation is like a two sided coin - heads is what you want, and tails is the lack of what you want. The key is to focus on what you actually want instead of the fact that you don't have it yet. Here's an example:

Emma's students are horrible. They don't listen to her, they talk during her lessons, they get into fights, and they cheat on tests. Emma dreads going to school every day, and is counting down the years until retirement. She complains to her coworkers in the lunchroom every day about her students and how awful they are.

Emma is focusing on all the negative aspects of her class, therefore she is vibrating at a low frequency around the topic. Although this is not what she consciously wants, her vibration is telling the Universe to bring her more disrespectful students and unpleasant experiences. If Emma focused, even for just 68 seconds at a time, on something positive about her class, her vibration would start to shift and she would start calling in more positive experiences.

Observe your thoughts and feelings from an objective place. Are most of your thoughts negative? Repeating phrases such as "Everything always goes wrong!" "Of course this would happen to me!" "Life is hard!" or "It's always something!" tells the Universe that you want more of whatever negative thing happened to you, because like attracts like - the Universe is bringing you more of what you are putting out.

How do you change these beliefs and thought patterns?

1. Start by making a note of every negative thought you have for a day or two. Don't judge it, just note how often your thoughts are focused on something you do NOT want in your reality.

2. When you are aware of your negative thoughts and are able to catch yourself having them, think three positive thoughts about what you do want in its place.

For active visualization, follow these steps:

1. Decide what you want - a peaceful class, a healthy body, a loving relationship, a million dollars...it can be anything!

2. Think about what that looks like, sounds like, smells like, feels like, tastes like. Get every detail in place.

3. Close your eyes and visualize the image of what you want in your head, then add in the secret sauce: FEEL what it feels like to already have what you want. Feel the peace, the joy, the security, the energy...whatever it is, feel what it feels like to already have it.

4. Hold onto this visualization for 68 seconds. Visualizing something for just 17 seconds is enough to activate that desire in the

The Aligned Teacher

Universe, but focusing on it for 68 seconds activates momentum and the process of bringing you your desire.

5. You can do this almost anywhere - before you get out of bed in the morning, sitting on the toilet, during your plan period, waiting in a carpool line. Any time you have a minute with nothing to do, visualize what you want in your life and feel the pure joy of already having it. Remember, feeling resentful that you don't physically have it yet will keep you in the place of not having it, so allow yourself to feel all the good feelings! After all, that's what we are really after anyway, isn't it?

Essential Oils

Essential oils have become much more mainstream, and even trendy, over the last several years. But essential oils are anything but new - people have been using them for centuries, with references to them in biblical texts. There are many aspects of essential oils I could get into, but I'm going to focus this particular discussion on how to best utilize them for teachers.

Before we get into that, I will give you a brief introduction in case you are unfamiliar with what essential oils are. Essential oils are volatile, aromatic compounds found on various parts of plants, or in layman's terms, they are the smelly part of plants. If you have ever smelled a flower or noticed that your hands smell like the orange you just peeled, you have experienced essential oils. Essential oils can be found on all parts of plants - the roots, the stems, the leaves, the buds, the flowers, the fruit. Essential oils are there for the plant's protection

The Aligned Teacher

– they have special mechanisms to help the plant heal itself. Because plants and people are both carbon based, people are able to utilize the benefits of the essential oil without the side effects that we often get from synthetic products.

There are many physical benefits to using essential oils (helping digestion, relieving sore muscles, etc.), but essential oils also carry many emotional and spiritual benefits. While there are several ways to use essential oils, aromatic use is the most effective for emotional support. Smelling an essential oil can be calming and soothing, uplifting and refreshing, or grounding and comforting. This happens because of the chemical response that occurs when the scent of the oil interacts with your limbic system, the part of the brain that stores your memories and controls behavioral and emotional responses.

Before I share ways to aromatically use essential oils for teachers, I must share that I specifically use dōTERRA Essential Oils for two reasons: The first is that dōTERRA puts a significant amount of resources into the science behind their oils - they have the most thorough testing for purity, potency and consistency on the market, while working with doctors, hospitals and universities studying the benefits and efficacy of their oils. From a scientific standpoint, they are the leaders in the field. The second reason is dōTERRA's humanitarian efforts with their Co-Impact Sourcing initiative, as well as their nonprofit Healing Hands Foundation. dōTERRA works to make the world a better place by providing well-paying jobs, schools, medical care, and clean water in underprivileged countries all over the world. I am sharing this with you because most essential oil companies do not meet these standards, and can legally contain fillers and impurities despite what their label says. When I make recommendations, I am specifically recommending dōTERRA oils. If you prefer another brand, that is fine and completely your choice, but please make sure you do your research on brands. While I am all for a good bargain, essential oils are not the place to look for the cheapest option, as what you breathe or use topically directly impacts your health.

There are several ways to use essential oils aromatically:

1. Diffusers - You can buy a diffuser from many places, this is not something that must be a specific brand. You can get them online or even at a health food store. A diffuser is a machine that you add water and a couple drops of oil to. When you turn it on, it will put out a fine mist with the scent of the oil. This is a great alternative to air fresheners or scented candles, which contain toxic ingredients and can have harmful health effects. Diffusers can help eliminate odors (hello middle and high school teachers!), as well as set the tone of the room.

2. If you don't have a diffuser, but want to give your mood a makeover, you can simply put a drop of oil in your hands, rub them together, cup them over your nose and mouth, close your eyes and inhale deeply a few times. This method is very effective at

getting the oils straight into your limbic system, as well as opening up nasal passages. Make sure you don't touch your face when you do this!

3. If you want to open up the airways in your lungs, put a drop of peppermint oil on your hands and rub them together. Hold one hand flat and make a circle with your other hand. Hold the circle against the palm of your other hand, put it up to your lips, and inhale deeply through your mouth.

Essential Oil Recommendations:

1. To support your immune system and keep those sniffles at bay (because who wants to write sub plans?), diffuse dōTERRA's On Guard blend, lemon, wild orange, frankincense, or clove oil in the classroom, at home, or even while you're sleeping. Oregano is another powerful immune supporter, but a lot of people think it's stinky in the diffuser, so you might save that one for bedtime!

2. For general stress relief or to calm down wild kids, diffuse lavender, wild orange, bergamot, lemon, rose, dōTERRA's Balance blend, dōTERRA's Serenity blend, or dōTERRA's Adaptiv blend.

3. For focus and concentration, diffuse lemon, peppermint or rosemary. dōTERRA's In Tune and Thinker blends come in rollers

that are difficult to diffuse, but can be used topically on the back of the neck, forehead and wrists (apply to the wrists and then smell your wrist for aromatic use). Pro tip: smelling the same scent while learning new material and being tested on it improves recall of information!

4. For anxious feelings, diffuse dōTERRA's Adaptiv blend. They also have a roller for topical use, as well as a capsule for internal use.

5. To neutralize odors in a stinky classroom, diffuse lemon or dōTERRA's Purify blend.

Safety Tips:

Essential oils are very powerful, and should be used with guidance (another reason to not just buy oregano oil at the grocery store). The following are important tips to remember when using essential oils:

1. Diffusing essential oils is generally a safe practice. Be sure to clean your diffuser with white vinegar and water to avoid mildew buildup.

2. Photosensitivity - Citrus oils (lemon, orange, bergamot, lime, etc.) are photosensitive. That means if you put them on topically

The Aligned Teacher

and then go in the sun or a tanning bed, you will burn in that area. If using citrus oils topically, be sure to put them in a place where the sun don't shine! (i.e. under clothing or the bottoms of your feet)

3. Diluting - If you have sensitive skin or are using essential oils topically on children or the elderly, be sure to dilute them in a carrier oil. Carrier oils are plant based oils like coconut, olive, avocado, grapeseed, or jojoba. Mix 1-2 drops of essential oil with 1 teaspoon of carrier oil. Do not use water to dilute essential oils! Water and oil don't mix, meaning the water will drive the oil further into the skin and cause a reaction. If you put an essential oil on your skin and it is burning, apply a carrier oil on top to soothe the situation.

4. Oil in the eye or other sensitive areas - This happens to the best of us! If you are handling an essential oil and then touch your eye, as mentioned earlier, DO NOT flush it out with water! Flush your eye out with a carrier oil or put some carrier oil on a tissue and wipe it on your eye. It should feel better in a few minutes. If the stinging persists, seek medical attention.

5. Hot oils - Some oils are considered "hot oils," including oregano, thyme, cinnamon, cassia, clove, and sometimes peppermint. These oils WILL cause skin sensitivity, no matter how tough you are. ALWAYS dilute these oils for topical use!

One last note is to make sure that you have permission from your administrators to diffuse essential oils in the classroom. Some schools do not allow this. If this is the case, you can still use them at home or apply them to yourself topically. Never apply an essential oil to a student without parental consent.

If you are interested in purchasing essential oils or having a free consultation with me, please see my website in the Resources section of this book.

Grounding

Grounding is a way to realign your energy and help you electrically reconnect to the Earth. When we are stressed or feeling frazzled, our energy can feel frantic. When in uncomfortable situations, it can be difficult for our Spirit to want to stay in the body, and it can disconnect a bit. This is very common and different from the Spirit leaving the body at the time of death. Grounding helps the Spirit drop back into the body so we are fully present in our lives.

There are several ways to Ground:

1. Do a grounding meditation. This can be a guided meditation or you can visualize it on your own. A grounding meditation typically includes visualizing a light coming in through the top of your head, slowly filling your body, and shooting out the bottom of your feet, going down to the center of the Earth, then

The Aligned Teacher

coming back up and out the crown of your head in a cycle. You could also visualize yourself as a tree, with roots growing out the bottom of your feet and stabilizing you into the Earth. Walk barefoot in the grass, dirt or sand outside. Hug a tree. Stand in the rain. Make any sort of physical contact with nature. Connecting your body with nature helps to reestablish that electrical connection that will help you feel more balanced and aligned.

2. Use doTERRA's Balance or Anchor blends. These blends are both designed to help you feel calm, peaceful and grounded. You can diffuse them, or use them topically on the bottom of your feet, in the navel, or over your heart.

16

Stomping in the Grass

Stomping in the grass is another form of grounding, but I wanted to make sure this one caught your eye! Stomping in the grass is a great thing to do to get rid of excess energy, especially anger and frustration. When you are really angry, people will tell you to scream or punch a pillow as healthy ways to get out your anger. Why does this work? Because you are releasing the angry energy from your body. Remember how we talked about energy transferring from one object to another? When you yell, hit something, or stomp, you are transferring that anger out of your body and into something else. You are releasing it. That's why it helps you feel better. We have to be careful, though, not to transfer our anger into another person. Yelling at a person, even if they are the ones who made us angry, only perpetuates the cycle of anger and belittling. Getting your anger and frustration out first allows you to have a calm and productive conversation with the person you are angry with and come to a peaceful resolution.

The Aligned Teacher

This technique is not reserved solely for anger and frustration. Stomping in the grass is a great way to release any energy that you accidentally picked up throughout your day, as well as energy that is no longer serving your highest good. Before you start, simply set the intention that you are releasing all energy that does not belong to you and that is no longer serving you.

Stomping in the grass is a wonderful option due to the transference of energy. The Earth is able to transmute our energy so that it can do no harm. The Earth knows what to do. If you don't have a patch of grass, dirt or sand nearby, you can stomp indoors or on a parking lot, simply set the intention that the energy is going through the floor to the earth to be transmuted.

This is a great routine to do every day after school when you are walking to your car. You could even meet several coworkers outside and stomp it out together. While you're at it, turn on some music and have a stomping party!

Stomping in the grass is another great tip to teach your students. Talk about how and why to do it before the kids are feeling frustration, anger, etc. so they understand the concept. Then encourage them to stomp it out while they're at recess as a way to refresh their day.

Salt

Sea salt (not table salt) absorbs and repels negative energies in your space or that have attached to your energy field. Have you ever noticed that you just feel happier at the beach? All that salt from the ocean permeates the whole atmosphere, allowing you to feel grounded, peaceful and happy. My favorite salt story is from my friend, Lindsay Marino, who used to teach third grade. She had a parent who would come barging into her classroom on a regular basis and disrupt her class. One day, she put salt across the threshold of her door. That afternoon, the parent still came, but instead of barging into the classroom, they poked their head in the door, keeping their feet firmly outside in the hallway! The salt created a barrier of protection for her classroom to keep the unhappy parent outside.

Here are some ways to utilize the energy neutralizing properties of salt:

The Aligned Teacher

1. Dissolve sea salt in a spray bottle with water and mist it in the air.

2. Place a thin line of salt along the doorway to your classroom or the entrances to your home.

3. Place bowls of salt water in your classroom (in a place where they won't get knocked over). Change this out every couple of days.

4. Get a Himalayan Salt Lamp for your classroom. Not only does this provide the benefits of the salt, but it is also visually calming to look at. Personally, it reminds me of relaxing at the spa!

5. Take a salt bath. Be sure to use sea salt to absorb any negative energies off of you. Feel free to also add two cups of Epsom salts. Epsom salt does not have the same energetic effect, but is a great way to soothe sore or tired muscles and give yourself a good dose of magnesium, which most people are deficient in. If you would like to add essential oils to your bath, be sure to put them in the salts rather than dropping them in the water. This way, they will get infused into the bath water as opposed to floating on top since oil and water do not mix.

Feng Shui

Your environment plays a big role in how you feel and how energy flows in your life. Feng Shui is an ancient Chinese energy system that, when used intentionally, allows your spaces and belongings to affect your life in a positive way. Everything around you affects your subconscious mind constantly, even if you are not aware of it. Being surrounded by clutter and items that are no longer in use, are broken, or remind you of negative memories keep the energy of your space stagnant and stale. It makes it harder to focus and can even cause anxiety and other health issues. This even affects you when you are not in that space. Think about the major spaces in your life - your home, your classroom, your car... are they neat and tidy, or cluttered and full of trash? You spend a good portion of your life in these spaces. They should feel good and supportive to you.

The first place to start for positive energy flow is with decluttering.

The Aligned Teacher

Clearing your space of things that you are no longer using releases lots of old, stuck energy, allowing the energy to flow more freely. Do you still have all your lesson plans from two curriculums ago that you will never use again? I know it can be difficult to get rid of something that you worked so hard on, but if you no longer need it, release it to allow for something new to come in. Make sure your desk is clean and tidy (something I never had when I was in the classroom!). Have students pick up after themselves, make sure there are no papers on the floor, and teach them how to keep their spaces tidy.

Once you have decluttered, then you can focus on furniture placement, colors, etc. Feng Shui has something called the Bagua Map, which is a 3x3 square map you can overlay on your space. Each square represents a different sector, including career, love and romantic relationships, family, wealth and prosperity, health, children and creativity, travel, knowledge and self-cultivation, and fame and reputation. Each sector has different elements (wood, metal, fire, water, earth) and colors that support that area. For example, black, dark grey and navy blue are considered water colors. Using these colors in the career sector are supportive, because the career sector's element is water. However, using these colors in the fame and reputation sector, whose element is fire, would not be helpful because water puts out fire.

If arranging, decorating, and decluttering comes easily, that is fantastic, and applying the principles of Feng Shui may seem like a piece of

Meredith Ruben Daniels

cake! There is another group of people, however, who struggle with decluttering, organizing and decorating. I fall into the latter category. The idea of Feng Shui was dropped into my life several times, catching my interest. However, decluttering and interior design are NOT my fortes. When we bought our house (before I knew all this information), we never painted the walls or invested in decorating much because I was scared to do it wrong, even though there were many parts of our house we wanted to change. After a year and a half of quarantines and virtual learning, I couldn't stand it anymore, and told Kevin that we needed to make some changes in the house. My biggest fear was spending a ton of money to redecorate, only to find out later that all of our changes were working against us. I decided to hire a Feng Shui consultant, Gina, to help us out. Gina gave us a full report on how to apply Feng Shui to our house, and we were able to make a lot of changes.

I resisted taking charge of my environment for years, thinking that clutter was just part of who I am and how I function. As time has gone on, I've started realizing how clutter affects my energy and mood. There are many external factors in our lives that we can't control, but our home and classroom are areas we can. Your students and family will also feel the difference and be grateful for a space where energy, peace and abundance flow freely.

If you are only wanting to apply Feng Shui to your classroom, or aren't wanting to invest in a personal consultant, there are plenty of

The Aligned Teacher

YouTube videos, internet articles, and people to follow on social media that can help you out. If you would like to work with Gina, you can find her website in the Resources section at the end of this book.

19

Acupressure Points

Receiving acupuncture is a wonderful way to align your energy; relieve stress and anxiety; and help improve your mood. It can also have other health benefits, such as relieving headaches and other chronic health issues. Acupuncture is the ancient Chinese art of placing thin, tiny needles in the skin on specific points to correct or clear energy blockages and restore optimal health. According to traditional Chinese medicine, the body has 2,000 acupressure points. These points align with the meridians, which as we talked about earlier, are pathways on the body that allow your vital life force energy, or "chi," to flow.

The best case scenario would be to work with an acupuncturist who knows how to address your specific and changing needs. However, if acupuncture is not in your budget or you don't like the idea of the needles, stimulating acupressure points on your body can be equally

The Aligned Teacher

effective. All you need to do is rub the spots gently for at least 15 seconds. Depending on how stressed you are, the points might be tender. This is a sign that you need to address that area. Again, there are great videos on the internet that can help you find the right points to rub based on what you are experiencing on a particular day.

If you are stuck in the classroom or can't look up a video, the following are some generalized acupressure points that you can rub throughout the day when you are feeling stressed or needing to protect your energy.

1. The crease on the underside of the elbow, on both sides. This is easy to do discreetly by crossing your arms across your chest.

2. Underneath the notches in your collar bone, both sides. Use your thumb and first finger to rub these spots.

3. Center of the sternum - place your hand on your chest with your thumb at the collar bone. Rub the spot in the center of your chest under your pinky finger. **Only do this at the end of the work day or later in the evening!

4. Top center of the head. **Only do this right before bed!

Breathwork

As we have discussed previously, when we feel anxious, angry, or upset, it has a physiological effect on our bodies. Our fight, flight or freeze reaction is triggered, our palms get sweaty, our stomachs tie up in knots, our breathing quickens and our hearts race. Cortisol, the stress hormone, is released into our bodies. While this is uncomfortable in the moment, the recurrent cycling of these events can lead to long term, chronic health problems.

We do not have conscious control over most of our organs. We don't think about which hormones we want our bodies to release and when; our food is going to digest whether we think about it or not. But there is one body system that we can consciously control - our breathing. When we choose to consciously control our breathing, it can affect the other parts of our bodies, including slowing the heart rate, relaxing our muscles, and balancing our stress hormones. By using a

The Aligned Teacher

Breathwork technique for a few minutes, you can shift your thoughts, your mood, and your body to be in a calmer, healthier state. The best part is, you are breathing all the time anyway, so you can literally do this anywhere, at any time, no special equipment necessary!

There are many different breathing techniques you can try. With any of these techniques, I recommend you focus on feeling your breath in your body. While most techniques require feeling your breath in your belly, some might focus on feeling it in the lungs or the back of the throat.

Here are a few basic Breathwork techniques. If you are looking for something more specific, as always, there are plenty of videos you can find online.

1. The Relaxing Breath, or 4-7-8 Breath by Dr. Andrew Weil, helps relax and calm the body. To do this breath, you will inhale through your nose to the count of 4, visualizing peace, love, or whatever feels nourishing to you flowing into your body. You will then hold your breath for 7 seconds before exhaling through your mouth for 8 seconds, releasing any excess energy that is no longer serving you.

2. For an energy boost, use Box Breathing, or the 4-4-4-4 technique. Box Breathing originated with the Navy Seals as a way to slow the heart rate, deepen concentration, and improve performance.

To do this breath, breathe in through the nose for 4 seconds, hold your breath in for 4 seconds, exhale through the nose for 4 seconds, and hold your breath out for 4 seconds. You can use the same visualizations as the 4-7-8 breath during the inhales and exhales.

3. The Conscious Breath, by Christine Day, involves taking a deep breath in and out through the mouth, with your mouth wide open. You may make a sound on the exhale involuntarily. The Conscious Breath helps with letting go - letting go of stress, of fear, even of illness. You can take a Conscious breath every ten minutes, every hour, or a couple times per day. More information about the Conscious Breath can be found in the Resources section.

Crystals

Crystals are a wonderful tool to help manage stress. I'm sure some of you are thinking that this is way too hippie dippy for you, and if so, that's totally fine, but hear me out first. I'm going to discuss two ways to use crystals - I'll start with the non-hippie way first!

Crystals are a part of nature. Bringing nature indoors is a way to help us feel grounded and connected to the great outdoors while enjoying the delight that is air conditioning. Simply having a bowl of crystals on a table or a few loose stones by your computer can be a reminder to slow down, take a deep breath and relax. If you experience a lot of anxiety, it can be very soothing to keep a crystal in your pocket and rub it throughout the day. Remember when you were a kid and you found a box of smooth crystals or rocks at a gift shop? That was definitely the coolest thing in the store, and it felt so good to stick

The Aligned Teacher

your hand in that big pile of cool stones, right? Kids love rocks! Use this to your advantage as a way to help calm students down. Keep a bowl with a variety of crystals in your classroom. When a student gets upset, allow them to go through the bowl, pick whichever one is speaking to them at that moment, and let them hold it for the rest of class. Just be sure to have strict rules that the crystals are for holding, not for throwing, and use discretion if a student has violent tendencies - crystals are for healing, not for hurting!

As for the "woo woo" reasons to use crystals, crystals hold a certain vibration, just like everything else in the world. Different crystals vibrate differently, and give off vibrations of love, peace and calming that we can pick up on when we are close to them. Other crystals, typically the black ones, have protective energy and can absorb negative energy around us.

There are different ways to utilize crystals as a teacher.

1. Keep one or two in your pocket (hard core crystal users will even keep some in their bra so they are close to the heart chakra). Rub them when you feel anxious (maybe not the one in your bra!).

2. Keep a bowl of smaller crystals on your desk or a table for ambiance or for students to hold when they need to relax.

3. Put larger crystals on display in the room. These can also be

examined with a magnifying glass if you need a quick science lesson.

4. Wear crystal jewelry. This is an easy way to keep the crystals on you while sharing their beauty.

You might be wondering how to know which crystals would be best for you. Here is a brief list of some common crystals and their properties:

1. Rose Quartz - This pink crystal promotes feelings of trust, harmony and love. While it does cover romantic love, rose quartz also promotes loving relationships amongst family members, with your students, with the world and with yourself.

2. Amethyst - This purple crystal is often used for spirituality and connection with Source, making it a beautiful crystal to use in meditation. Amethyst is also said to assist with supporting the immune system, deep sleep, and migraines.

3. Citrine - This yellow crystal helps promote health, wealth and guards against negative vibrations. Citrine is known for bringing positivity to tough situations and helping uplift your mood.

4. Black Tourmaline - Black Tourmaline helps you to stay grounded and absorbs toxic vibrations around you. This crystal is often

used to help people reduce their sad and anxious feelings.

If you would like more information on crystals, you can click the link in the Resources section of this book.

Where should I get my crystals?

Crystals can be found in a variety of places, from crystal shows to metaphysical stores to Home Goods and TJ Maxx. There are many Etsy shops that sell them, as well. If possible, it's best to buy your crystals in person so you can pick them up and feel the vibration of each one. If that's not possible, ask the seller questions to ensure that you are working with a reputable dealer.

If you are looking for crystal jewelry, I highly recommend Squeen's Beads. Sarah, the owner of this shop is a single mom who makes fabulous crystal jewelry infused with Reiki energy. Check out her Facebook group in the Resources section.

Sound Healing

"Future medicine will be the medicine of frequencies."
- Albert Einstein

Sound is another type of energy that has an effect on our bodies, minds, and spirits. I'm sure you have a favorite song (or several) that always puts you in a good mood when you listen to it, right? Or maybe you have a playlist that you love to listen to on rainy days or when you want to chill out. Whatever mood you want to establish, there is a music genre to help you get there. Listening to music changes your vibration to match the vibration of the song. Listening to your favorite music on your way to or from school every day is a great way to put yourself in a good mood!

Sound healing expands on this concept. While all music and sound has a vibration to it, there are certain frequencies that help our bodies relax and heal. One of my very favorite things to do is have a sound bath - this is where you lay down, get comfortable, and a sound healer plays the crystal or metal singing bowls, lulling you into a deep state of relaxation. You relax so much that you are able to let go of tension, fear, or anxiety that you might be holding, allowing the cells of your body to breathe and heal. If you can find a sound healer close to you, I highly recommend trying a sound bath!

If you are unable to have a live sound bath, or even for when you are at home or in your classroom (your plan period would be a great time for this), you can find many different sound healing videos online. Depending on what you prefer, you can find a singing bowl sound bath, relaxing piano music (one of my favorites for working or just relaxing, I'm listening to it as I type this!), rain, ocean or nature sounds, or Solfeggio frequencies.

Solfeggio frequencies are specific frequencies shown to have positive effects on the body, mind and emotions. Listening to these frequencies while relaxing or sleeping can help reduce anxiety and provide a healing environment. Different frequencies have different properties to them:

174hz: Removes pain
285hz: Influences energy fields
396hz: Liberates you from fear and guilt
417hz: Facilitates change

432hz: Miracle tone of nature
528hz: Repairs DNA
639hz: Heals relationships
741hz: Awakens intuition
852hz: Attracts soul tribe
963hz: Connects with light and spirit

Another option for sound healing is to create the sound yourself using singing or toning. You can match your voice to specific pitches to create the frequency you desire. I believe this is particularly helpful, as you are expressing yourself and releasing energy and emotion through your voice.

If sound healing resonates with you, you could even look into getting a singing bowl to play for your students or at home. This would be a great way to start the day or to help students calm down when the energy gets too high or students are upset. You could even play it as a cue to your class that it's time to listen to you or to calm down. This would be a great tool for counselors to have in their offices, as well.

Forest Bathing

Spending time in nature is a wonderful way to de-stress. We've already talked about stomping in the grass and how having your bare feet on the earth can help pull negative energy out of your body to be transmuted, but there is more to it.

The Japanese coined a term called Shinrin-yoku, or forest bathing. While I typically think of bathing as getting clean and time in nature as getting dusty and sweaty (I will admit, I need to follow my own advice on this one and get outside more), Forest Bathing is about immersing yourself in the beauty that is nature. This is a time to leave your phone and camera at home (or on silent in your pocket if you need it for safety purposes) and be truly present.

Find a park, forest, or garden, and simply be. This is not about working up a sweat and getting your heart rate up. Slowly meander through the trees or down a path. Feel the sun on your skin, observe how it streams through the leaves and notice what it shines on. Take deep breaths and smell the scent of the trees. Listen to the birds chirp and the leaves rustle in the breeze. Sit on a rock or by a stream and simply observe nature. You can even meditate or do yoga, art or another favorite activity outside.

While many people only want to spend time outside in moderate weather, you can truly spend time in nature any time of the year. A friend once told me, "There's no such thing as bad weather, you just need to have the right clothing!" Feel the rain on your skin without panicking that you need to get inside or pull out your umbrella. Just dance in the rain, whether by yourself, with a partner, or your kids. You can even watch the weather forecast and plan an outdoor dance party for the next time it rains! When you come inside, put on warm, snuggly clothes, make a cup of hot chocolate, and watch your favorite movie!

Like everything else we've discussed, nature is wonderful for your students, too. Does your school have an outside nature area or garden where you can go to teach? Getting outside for learning time, to work on a project, or for a read aloud, is a great way to give your students some fresh air and help them enjoy the benefits and beauty of nature. Nature in itself is an incredible learning tool, so incorporate it into your lesson plans and get out there as often as possible!

You can also bring nature into your classroom. Bringing in plants, crystals, even an herb garden to keep by the window will help you and your students enjoy the benefits of nature all day long. You can even find some plants that are good at cleaning the air to promote a healthy classroom environment.

If relaxation isn't enough reason to make you want to spend time in nature, there are also proven health benefits. Many hospitals incorporate nature into their decor, as they have found better health outcomes for their patients. Studies have been done on issues like cardiovascular and metabolic health, hypertension, psychological issues and even the anti-cancer benefits of forest bathing. You can find these studies in the Resources section.

Final Thoughts

Teachers are one of our most valuable resources. You dedicate your lives to helping our children learn and grow, and therefore, help our world become a better place. You deserve to be happy. You deserve to relax. You deserve to feel at peace. While I can't solve the problem of kids playing on their cell phones in class, it is my true hope that at least one technique that I shared with you in this book will help you and your students find more peace, love and joy in life.

Being a teacher is part of who you are, but you are so much more than that. Your family and friends love you and want you to play full out in life with them. The world needs you to show up as your whole self, shining your light brightly. Incorporating some of these modalities into your daily routine can help dust off the cobwebs of stress and anxiety and allow you to shine for the world.

It is clear that the system of education has a lot of problems and needs a good revamp. Having happy, balanced teachers who are able to teach healthy emotional regulation to their students is a key component in helping us get where we need to be. It is my sincere hope that the techniques in this book will start a revolution of emotional health in our schools.

If you would like some daily accountability and support to help you incorporate the practices from this book into your daily routine, please join my free Facebook group, The Aligned Teacher Community. I post daily prompts to help you keep a positive mindset throughout the school year. The exercises in this book are not a one and done activity – they must be practiced daily to truly make a difference in your life. Having a community of people who are on the same journey as you is also invaluable – it is much easier to stay positive when surrounded by other positive people. The Resources section contains a link to the group.

I can't thank you enough for all you do for your students and our communities as a whole.

You are worthy.
You are valued.
You are loved.

Sending you all my wishes for the best school year ever,

Meredith

RESOURCES

If you would like Meredith Ruben Daniels to speak at a professional development day or to work with her in another capacity, you may reach her at: www.soulful-wellness.com

The following links may be helpful if you wish to look further into a particular topic:

1. The Aligned Teacher Community Facebook Group: https://www.facebook.com/groups/625335005640496

2. Marilyn Eagen: https://marilyneagen.com/

3. Eden Energy Medicine: https://edenmethod.com/

4. Hook Up Demonstration: https://www.youtube.com/watch?v=I0N7gTuhXXg

5. Triple Warmer Smoothie Demonstration: Meditation: https://www.healthline.com/health/9-ways-to-make-meditation-easier

The Aligned Teacher

6. Emotional Freedom Technique with Michelle Woodruff: www.magicmichellewoodruff.com

7. Purchase doTERRA Essential Oils: www.my.doterra.com/meredithrubendaniels or www.soulful-wellness.com to schedule a consultation

8. Put Your Worries Down Guided Meditation: https://www.soulful-wellness.com/guided-meditation

9. Feng Shui with Gina Ballard: www.ginanicole.net

10. Read about the Conscious Breath: https://www.edgemagazine.net/2019/08/the-conscious-breath/

11. Information about Crystals: https://tinyrituals.co/blogs/tiny-rituals/healing-crystal-guide-essential-gemstones#Rose-Quartz

12. Squeen's Beads Facebook Group: https://www.facebook.com/squeensbeads

Meredith Ruben Daniels

ABOUT THE AUTHOR

Meredith Ruben Daniels received her B.S. in Elementary and Early Childhood Education from the University of Wisconsin-Madison and her M.A. in Teaching from Missouri Baptist University. She spent nine years in the classroom. Meredith's spiritual journey began with the passing of her father, and she has since become a Certified Generational Emotional Mapping Ancestral Healer, Reiki Master, Psychic Medium, dōTERRA Wellness Advocate, speaker, and co-author of the best-selling book, Energy Healing and Soul Medicine. Teachers have always held a special place in Meredith's heart, and she has found a passion in sharing her knowledge of energy work with teachers to help them reduce stress and feel happier in both the classroom and their everyday lives. Meredith would love to present this information at your school for professional development.

Meredith lives in St. Louis, MO with her husband, Kevin, and their three boys. In her spare time, you can find Meredith at her kids' activities or sitting in a carpool line.

Made in the USA
Monee, IL
06 September 2023